Getting Green Now

Tips For A Greener Life Quick

Kim Cecchi

authorHOUSE®

AuthorHouse™
1663 Liberty Drive
Bloomington, IN 47403
www.authorhouse.com
Phone: 1-800-839-8640

Published by AuthorHouse   2/16/2012

ISBN: 978-1-4685-3475-7 (sc)
ISBN: 978-1-4685-3474-0 (e)
This e-book helps save trees.

Library of Congress Control Number: 2011963470

Thank you

Special thanks and much love go out to Kristine Lambert and Laura Hirsch, for helping me edit this book and for their valued insights. Having a fresh pair of eyes is always helpful and very much appreciated.

I would also like to thank the many companies and organizations that provided the research and information that made the writing of this book possible.

Kim Cecchi ☺

Table of Contents

The Purpose of this book

I wrote this book with the intention of helping those who are unaware of how the things they may do in their daily lives impact the health of people and our planet to make better choices.

You will receive quick tips on what you can do to "green" your lifestyle, and why it is a good idea to do things a little different.

Some chapters have a tip that is similar to one in a different section. I did this in case you skipped another chapter, but the tip is also relevant in that section.

Start slowly, maybe picking 5 or 10 tips, and make the change. After you have become comfortable with the changes, change a few more things.

Before you know it, you will be **GREEN**!

Then, start to spread the word!

Green Home

1. Tip: Recycle whenever you can.

   Why? Recycling will reduce the amount of waste you send to landfills by around 75 percent and reduce the amount of resources used to make the product. Recycle paper, plastic, aluminum, glass, and electronics whenever you can. Check out the website www.earth911.com . ☺

2. Tip: Switch to energy-saving light-bulbs.

   Why? Compact fluorescent light-bulbs (CFL) and Light Emitting Diodes (LED) light-bulbs use 75% less energy and last about 10 times as long as incandescent bulbs. Switching will keep a lot of greenhouse gasses out of the air, and will save you money.
   Try www.philips.com.

3. Tip: Shorten your showers.

   Why? You can save more than 5 gallons of water for every minute you shorten your shower. Limit showers to 5 minutes or less. Set a timer if it helps.

4. Tip: Try reed aromatherapy diffusers with essential oils to give your home a constant fragrance.

Why? They work like other air fresheners, like plug-ins, but don't waste energy, last longer, and don't contain nasty chemicals, like phthalates. Try www.wholesalereeddiffusers.com.

5. Tip: Use natural cleaners.

Why? They don't have toxins in them, work well, and cost less. Try making your own from vinegar, baking soda, and borax.

6. Tip: Wash your clothes in cold water.

Why? Ninety percent of the energy used by your washing machine goes to heating up the water. They will get just as clean as using hot water, and will save you money.

7. Tip: Use an earth-friendly laundry detergent. You can also make your own detergent. Start by soaking the clothes in a bucket half full of water and ½ cup of lemon juice before you wash the load in the washing machine. Add ¼ cup of baking soda to brighten and ¼ of vinegar to soften the clothes.

Why? Your clothes are not really clean if you wash them in chemicals. They can damage your health and the environment. Check out www.seventhgeneration.com and www.Ecover.com.

8. Tip: Install low-flow water-heads.

Why? You will reduce the amount of water you use while you shower and your water bill will be less. Try www.oxygenics.com, www.homedepot.com, www.watersavertech.com, and www.caromausa.com.

9. Tip: Turn off the water when you brush your teeth.

Why? All that clean water is going right down the drain and being wasted.

10. Tip: Use fans instead of air conditioning.

Why? Portable and ceiling fans use 90 percent less energy than central air. You also will save money on your electric bill.

11. Tip: Skip the dryer sheets.

Why? They have toxic chemicals in them, clog your lint trap, waste trees, waste money, and end up in a landfill. ☹ If you must, try www.seventhgeneration.com.

12. Tip: Clean chrome with a rub made from 2 tbsp. of salt and 1 tsp. of white vinegar.

Why? It is non-toxic and will make your chrome sparkle!

13. Tip: Keep the heat and air conditioning down.

Why? For every degree you lower the thermostat when it is cold, you can save 1-3 % on your heating bill, and the reverse is true for air-conditioning. Shoot for 68 degrees in the winter and 78 degrees in the summer. Programmable thermostats are great for controlling the temperature of your home.

14. Tip: Turn the thermostat way down at night when it is cold. Shoot for 60-62 degrees.

Why? You will use a lot less energy and money. Pile up the blankets or get an electric blanket, hot water bottle, or space heater.

15. Tip: Don't use bleach to clean your clothes.

Why? Bleach can irritate skin and the fumes are toxic. Try hydrogen peroxide, baking soda, or white distilled vinegar.

16. Tip: Use natural shower curtains made from organic cotton or bamboo.

Why? They are made from natural and renewable materials. Vinyl shower curtains contain polyvinyl chloride (PVC) and DEHP, a phthalate suspected of causing hormonal disruption, and a carcinogen. Keep these nasties out of our landfills and water supplies. An EPA study found that vinyl shower curtains can elevate air toxins in your home for more than a month. Check out www.healthgoods. com and PVC-free curtains at www.jcp.com.

17. Tip: Reduce your indoor air pollution by ventilating your home.

Why? Indoor air pollution can be 2 to 5 times more polluted than outdoor air, according to the Environmental Protection Agency. Most of us spend 90% of our time indoors, so open some windows, get some plants, turn on some fans to circulate the air, and lose the toxic air fresheners and cleaning supplies.

18. Tip: Get rid of the ant traps.

Why? They are poison. Try hitting the affected areas with vinegar (my favorite), lemon juice, baking soda, cinnamon, or coffee grounds.

19. Tip: Unplug appliances when they are turned off.

Why? Plugged in appliances continue to draw electricity even when they are off. Energy Star says that in the average home, 40% of all electricity used to power home electronics is consumed while the products are turned off! You can use a power strip with as many electronics as you can and turn it off. Power strips don't continue to draw power when they are in the "off" position.

20. Tip: Use cloth napkins and towels instead of paper ones.

Why? They can be reused over and over, and you don't need trees chopped down to use them. If you do use paper towels and napkins, recycle them if they aren't too messy.

21. Tip: Hang-dry your clothes.

Why? You won't use any electricity or money, your clothes won't shrink, and they will look new longer. If they dry outside, they will smell super fresh! ☺

22. Tip: Buy rechargeable batteries.

Why? You can use them over and over again.

23. Tip: Wipe spills with cloth towels.

Why? They can be reused and washed instead of being thrown away.

24. Tip: Upgrade your furnace.

Why? They use less energy and save you money. Energy Star rated appliances are great. Check out the winner of their 2011 Emerging Technology Award at www. marathonengines.com for residential and commercial systems that are great for saving energy and keeping more of your money in your wallet. ☺

25. Tip: Seal drafts around your windows.

Why? It will save you money on your energy bills and keep your home warmer during the cold months.

26. Tip: Wrap your water heater and set the thermostat to 120 degrees.

Why? It will save you between 4% and 9% in water heating costs and reduce standby heat losses by 25% - 45%. A tank that is warm to the touch needs more insulation.

27. Tip: Get an energy audit.

Why? You will find out where you are losing energy in your home – then you can fix it right away.

28. Tip: Turn off the lights when you leave the room.

Why? It saves money, energy, and CO2 emissions.

29. Tip: Don't leave your outside lights on overnight, unless they are solar-powered.

Why? It wastes energy and money, and releases CO2 into the environment.

30. Tip: Install low-flow or dual flush toilets.

Why? You will use a lot less water, and save money.

31. Tip: Buy larger sizes of everyday items.

Why? They will last longer and cost less if you buy them in bulk, and you will save packaging, too.

32. Tip: Wipe windows clean with old newspapers.

Why? They clean great, and can be reused and recycled.

33. Tip: Use natural or organic cleaners.

Why? They don't contain nasty chemicals that will release toxins into your home and are often a lot cheaper.

34. Tip: Fix leaky faucets or pipe joints.

Why? One faulty faucet can waste 3 gallons of water per day, according to the U.S. Geological Survey.

35. Tip: Make your own cleaning solutions.

Why? They won't have any nasty chemicals in them and will save you money. I clean most things with a spray of vinegar and water ☺

36. Tip: The average tub faucet flows between three and five gallons of water per minute. Plug the drain in the tub or collect the cold water in a pitcher while the water warms up for your bath or shower.

Why? You won't let the water go down the drain, being wasted. Use the captured water for your plants, dishes, cleaning, or cooking.

37. Tip: Only fill your bath ¼ of the way full.

Why? If you prefer to take baths over showers, try to use the same amount of water you would use for a five-minute shower. The less water that goes down the drain, the better…especially the soapy kind.

38. Tip: Try to choose "green" products.

Why? They are better for your health and for the environment.

39. Tip: Get your home toxin-free.

Why? The health of your family and pets depends on it.

40. Tip: Compost.

Why? About 61 million tons of food scraps, yard trimmings, and shredded paper go into U.S. landfills every year. Adding compost to your garden will create nice, nutrient-rich topsoil and plants. It will also keep the garbage out of the landfill. You can purchase a composter at hardware and home-improvement stores or online. Try www.compostguide.com.

41. Tip: Only run your dishwasher and washing machine when they are full.

Why? You should save the water, money, and electricity until you actually need to use it.

42. Tip: Turn off the water while you scrub your dishes.

   Why? You are wasting the water going down the drain.

43. Tip: Don't use a garbage disposal.

   Why? Composting your food waste or throwing it away will save money on maintaining your septic system, will keep your drain less clogged, and prevent disruption of nutrient balances in soil and water ecosystems.

44. Tip: Use a microwave instead of an oven when possible.

   Why? Microwaves are between 3.5 and 4.8 times more energy efficient than your oven. Crock-pots are wonderful, too. In summer months your house will stay cooler with the oven being off.

45. Tip: Don't preheat your oven.

   Why? You will save about two kilowatt-hours of energy per hour your oven is not on and the time you waste waiting for it to warm up.

46. Tip: Make sure the refrigerator door is closed.

   Why? It will save you $30 to $60 per year on your electric bill. It is the kitchens biggest energy-consuming appliance – about 14 percent of a home's electricity.

47. Tip: Store leftovers in glass or porcelain containers.

Why? Plastic can leach chemicals into your food and cause health problems. Find glass food containers at www. ikea.com, www.bedbathandbeyond.com.

48. Tip: Install a water filter on your sink and get refillable water bottles.

Why? You will get clean, pure water and not have to recycle anymore plastic water bottles. Either re-use the plastic water bottles or get refillable bottles. Check out www.brita.com and www.purwater.com.

49. Tip: Turn the water off when you wash your face or shave.

Why? You will conserve up to 5 gallons of water per day. You can also brush your teeth while you wait for the water to warm to shave.

50. Tip: Flush your toilet less. Place waste, like tissues with dead spiders in them, in the trash, and if you go #1, flush it later.

Why? You'll save about 4.5 gallons of water per flush.

51. Tip: If you have a fireplace, keep the damper closed whenever there is not a fire in it.

Why? Around 8 percent of your home's heat can escape and cost you more money on your heating bill.

52. Tip: Close the curtains when it's cold or sunny.

Why? In the summer it keeps the house cool by blocking the sun, and in the winter it helps insulate the windows and keeping drafts out. Doing this could reduce your energy bills by around 25 percent.

53. Tip: Buy a permanent air filter for your furnace that can be cleaned and reused over and over again.

Why? Disposable filters need to be replaced several times a year, use resources to make, cost money, and end up in landfills.

54. Tip: Clean the lint screen in your dryer after each use.

Why? It conserves energy, saves cash, and reduces fire hazard. Keeping it clean decreases energy use by up to 30 percent.

55. Tip: Water your yard minimally.

Why? You can save up to 6.5 gallons of water per minute and save money on your water bill.

56. Tip: Turn your thermostat up or down 15-20 degrees when you are away from home – up in the summer, down in the winter. Turning it off completely will work sometimes, too.

Why? You will save a lot of energy, and some money.

57. Tip: Buy recycled toilet paper and tissues.

Why? It is made from recycled paper (not recycled toilet paper – yuck!), no nasty chemicals, such as chlorine, you save trees, and it is super soft. Check out <u>www. greenforest-products.com</u>.

58. Tip: Use voice-mail instead of an answering machine.

Why? Answering machines draw energy all the time, then, when they break down, they need to be recycled or end up in a landfill.

59. Tip: Buy block cheese instead of pre-sliced individually wrapped slices.

Why? You will save money, energy, and resources used in the production of the little wrappers they come in.

60. Tip: If you use paper towels instead of cloth towels, buy rolls that have been recycled and have smaller sheets.

Why? You will make the roll last longer, save money and resources, and have less waste.

61. Tip: Choose trash liner bags made from recycled materials.

Why? Their production requires less energy to manufacture.

62. Tip: Buy paper-wrapped soap instead of liquid soap in plastic bottles.

   Why? You will save money, packaging costs, and materials.

63. Tip: If you have a baby, use cloth diapers.

   Why? Disposable diapers use a lot of resources to make and then end up in the landfill. If you toss 4,000 diapers, that equals about 1,500 pounds of waste.

64. Tip: Buy liquid laundry detergent that is vegetable-based, not petroleum based.

   Why? They are better for you and they won't deplete our fossil fuel supply. Check out www.seventhgeneration.com

65. Tip: Get electronic bank statements and bank online.

   Why? You will save the paper, resources, and energy needed to make them, time, stamps, and gas going to the bank.

66. Tip: Make payments electronically.

   Why? You will save time, paper, stamps, and possibly late fees!

67. Tip: Get your tax refunds electronically.

Why? You will save the paper they are printed on, the envelopes they arrive in, the postage used to send them, and you will get your money around a month faster.

68. Tip: Buy carpet made from recycled materials.

Why? Synthetic fibers use more energy and let off toxic emissions. Plastic bottles can be recycled into carpet. ☺

69. Tip: If you are looking for new furniture, try to find some with recycled fabric.

Why? It will save on materials and energy used in production.

70. Tip: Use cut up old clothes to clean with.

Why? They can be reused over and over, you can wash them, and they will cost you nothing.

71. Tip: Cook at home instead of getting take-out.

Why? You save money, no non-recyclable containers to feel guilty about, and no plastic utensils and bags going to recycling or landfills.

72. Tip: Buy 100% recycled glass tiles for your kitchen remodel.

Why? You will save energy, materials, and money. Try www.ecospaces.net or www.mytilebacksplash.com.

73. Tip: Replacing your floors? Try bamboo.

Why? You will save many trees and resources. Bamboo is sustainable, beautiful, and affordable. Check out www.ambientbamboo.com and www.calibamboo.com.

74. Tip: Choose linoleum over vinyl flooring.

Why? Linoleum is produced from all-natural resources, while vinyl flooring is produced from plastic made from petroleum.

75. Tip: Select highly reflective roofing materials.

Why? You will save money and energy – 1,100 kilowatt-hours and $90 per year for cooling. Check out www.kellyroofing.com.

76. Tip: Choose insulation that has been recycled from denim, glass, newspaper, or other materials.

Why? Fiberglass insulation uses around 6 times more energy to produce than recycled materials. Try recycled denim insulation and make donations of your old jeans at www.greenjeaninsulation.com.

77. Tip: For outdoor lighting, install motion sensors.

Why? The lights will only turn on if something triggers it – saving you money and energy. Check out www.homedepot.com and www.lowes.com.

78. Tip: Install solar panels.

Why? Free energy from the sun! Also, you can get tax credits and rebates to help with the cost of the panels. Check out www.solar-werks.com, www.windycityrenewableenergy.com, and www.mrsolar.com.

79. Tip: Use recycled plastic lumber to build your deck.

Why? Treated wood can leach toxic chemicals into the soil and water supplies, you will keep plastic out of landfills, and you will save trees. Check out www.epsplasticlumber.com.

80. Tip: Plant shade trees on the east and west sides of your home.

Why? Lots of energy and money savings.

81. Tip: Plant a windbreak – a dense row of small trees and evergreen shrubs – on the west and north sides of your home.

WHY? It can reduce heating costs by around 1,400 kilowatt-hours and $110 a year.

82. Tip: Buy double-paned windows.

Why? You can save around $400 a year in energy costs.

83. Tip: Use non-toxic cleaning supplies.

WHY? The toxic fumes pollute your home and contribute to greenhouse gas emissions.

84. Tip: Any cleaning sprays that have bleach or are called antibacterial have got to go.

Why? Antibacterials contain triclosan, which, when exposed to chlorinated tap water, produces dangerous by-products. Chlorine bleach is a poisonous gas and a hazardous chemical, and could be toxic to the immune system and reproductive system, and cause neurological problems.

85. Tip: Make sure there are no phosphates in your laundry and dishwashing detergents.

Why? Phosphates cause a chain reaction connecting algae bloom consuming the phosphates drained into lakes and rivers, reproduction, microorganisms, reproduction, stripping the water of oxygen, and the lake or river drying up. Not good. ☹

86. Tip: Baking soda and vinegar work great for toilets.

WHY? They're natural, and work just as well as conventional toilet cleaners that may have bleach and other dangerous chemicals, such as naphthalene, a suspected carcinogen, in them. Sprinkle a little of each in the bowl, wait until it is done fizzing, then scrub. Super simple.

87. Tip: Use a bar of soap instead of antibacterial wipes or antibacterial soap.

WHY? Antibacterial soaps can contain some pretty harmful ingredients, like triclosan, and kill the germs we need to have a strong immune system.

88. Tip: Get some tea tree oil.

Why? It's a natural solvent that cuts grease, and kills bacteria and germs. It's good for cuts, put in shampoo for dandruff, and when it's diluted with water, it's a good mouthwash. Get the real thing – Melaleuca alternifolia, which has healing properties.

89. Tip: Clean with vinegar.

Why? It's the best natural cleaner (or one of the best). Use it as a drain cleaner, window cleaner, washing machine cleaner, etc. Go to www.vinegartips.com.

90. Tip: Use toothpaste to clean your silver.

Why? It works awesome and it doesn't have any nasty chemicals in it.

91. Tip: Clean the coils of your refrigerator.

   Why? Keeping them clean will save money and energy.

92. Tip: Instead of plastic wrap, put a plate or bowl over your leftovers in the fridge.

   Why? It saves resources and money, and the chemicals in the plastic won't get into your food.

93. Tip: Keep your bathroom well ventilated.

   Why? Chlorine gas is released in hot water. Chlorine bonds to the hair and skin, and can easily destroy their natural balance, causing itchiness, dryness, and flaking. Check out www.realgoods.com for chlorine filters.

94. Tip: Buy 100% organic cotton or bamboo towels.

   Why? Bamboo is a renewable resource, and cotton and bamboo are not grown with fertilizers or pesticides. Try www.gaiam.com, www.annasova.com, and www.looporganic.com for bamboo towels. Find bamboo washcloths at www.vivaterra.com and www.jcp.com.

95. Tip: Install faucet aerators.

   Why? They will cut your faucet water use by around 50 percent. You can find them at home improvement stores.

96. Tip: Check your toilet for leaks and flush less.

Why? You will save a ton of water. About 40% of the drinking water supplied to homes is flushed down the toilet.

97. Tip: Never use those blue toilet deodorizers.

Why? The nasty chemicals go into your drinking water, our lakes and streams, etc.

98. Tip: Get an air purifier.

Why? It cleans the air in your home with little electricity use.

99. Tip: Try a wool mattress.

Why? They are dust mite and mildew resistant, flame retardant, and they dry fast.

100. Tip: Get a battery-run alarm clock.

Why? You will save electricity and will not have the bright light in your room. Check out www.now-zen.com.

101. Tip: Get a solar-powered fan and skylight (to let the sun in) for your attic.

Why? It exhausts hot air from your attic without using any electricity. Check out www.sunrisesolar.net and www.bigfrogmountain.com.

102. Tip: Get a solar charger for cell phones.

Why? You will not use any electricity to charge the items you use regularly. Check out www.solio.com.

103. Tip: Let your faucet run, saving the water for plants, rinsing dishes, etc., for 20 seconds before drinking the water or cooking with it.

Why? Water can become polluted from sitting idle in the pipes, where toxic chemicals from the metal can seep in.

104. Tip: Wash new clothes before you wear them.

Why? Many clothes are made with toxic dyes that rub off on your skin and can be absorbed into your bloodstream. Better yet, buy organic clothes made with natural (plant based) dyes.

105. Tip: Reduce your tap water flow to a pencil-width stream when you turn on the water to wash something.

Why? A faucet that is on full stream can send three to five gallons of water down the drain in one minute. Two-thirds of the water can go down the drain. You will save resources and money by having a smaller stream.

106. Tip: Garden with mulch and native plants.

Why? Mulch reduces water evaporation, keeps the soil cool in the summer, and warm in the winter. Planting native species will also save water.

107. Tip: Open your dishwasher when it's done washing or turn off the drying cycle.

Why? Letting dishes air-dry saves energy and money.

108. Tip: Toss a few dry towels into the dryer when you run it.

Why? The towels pull moisture out of the wet clothes, reducing the time the dryer will run.

109. Tip: Get a hybrid grill with electric or gas as its main source of heat.

Why? It will save gas. Try www.kalamazoogourmet. com/hybrid.

110. Tip: Never microwave plastic or Styrofoam.

Why? They are made from petroleum and chemicals. Heating them up can cause transfer of toxic properties into the food. Use glass, Pyrex, or ceramic dishes.

111. Tip: Keep your refrigerator at 37 degrees F and your freezer at 3 degrees.

Why? Anything colder is overkill and a waste of energy.

112. Tip: Don't buy beverages in 2-liter plastic bottles.

Why? It takes 26 bottles of water to produce the plastic container for a 1-liter bottle, and doing so pollutes 25 liters of groundwater.

113. Tip: Supplement your heat with a wood pellet stove.

Why? They produce very little smoke and ash, and are more efficient than traditional fireplaces or wood stoves. The wood pellets are made out of recycled, compressed sawdust that would otherwise be thrown out by mills. Check out www.woodpelletstoves.net and www.harmanstoves.com.

114. Tip: Get your news online or from television.

Why? It saves resources, paper, petroleum, and the plastic bags they often come in.

115. Tip: Be more tolerant of a few wrinkles in your clothes- throw them in the dryer for a few minutes, or steam them as you shower.

Why? An iron uses around the same amount of energy as 10 100-watt light bulbs.

116. Tip: Take your clothes out of the dryer as soon as they are dry.

Why? They won't wrinkle.

117. Tip: Get a tank-less water heater.

Why? It heats when it is used – no waiting and water waste. Check out www.rinnai.us/tankless-water-heater/.

118. Tip: Buy bread wrapped in single wrappers.

Why? Double wrapping is a total waste of resources and energy.

119. Tip: Get a low-flow shower-head.

Why? It only uses 1.5 gallons of water per minute, saving water, and this will save you money.

120. Tip: Put a gallon jug full of water into your toilet tank.

Why? You will save a gallon of water with every flush and save money on your water bill.

121. Tip: Skip the fabric softener.

Why? They are made from animal fat. Yuck. Use vinegar instead.

122. Tip: Get cookware coated with thermalon instead of Teflon.

Why? The EPA is asking companies to phase out Teflon. The Environmental Working Group has shown that overheated non-stick pans emit a toxic mixture of chemicals that may cause cancer, birth defects, immune system suppression and increased risk of heart attack and stroke.

123. Tip: Buy concentrated formulas of laundry detergent, etc.

Why? You will save cash and there is less packaging to recycle because you buy fewer containers.

124. Tip: Don't use Nalgene water bottles.

Why? They are made from polycarbonate (#7 on the bottom), which may leach Bisphenol A, an estrogen-like chemical.

125. Tip: Buy drinks in glass containers.

Why? Producing typical #1 plastic water bottles produces a hundred times more pollution than manufacturing glass.

126. Tip: If you installed your toilet before 1994, it's time to upgrade.

Why? Many older toilets use 3.5 to 7 gallons of water per flush. Adding something weighted to the tank, a dual-flush toilet, and a low-flow or no-flow toilet will reduce the amount of water used.

127. Tip: Paint your roof white.

Why? White reflects heat, resulting in a cooling effect and reversing global warming.

128. Tip: When you take a bath, close the drain before turning on the water. Catch the cold water with a pitcher or two for your plants or cooking.

Why? You will save a lot of water.

129. Tip: If you are replacing your refrigerator, get an Energy Star qualified model with the freezer on top.

Why? Energy Star certified models are the most efficient. Models with the freezer on the top perform 10-25 percent more efficiently than side-by-side models.

130. Tip: Don't buy a refrigerator with ice makers and ice and water dispensers on the door.

Why? They increase the refrigerators use by 14-20 percent and raise the price of the unit itself by $75 to $250, according to the U.S. Department of Energy.

131. Tip: Keep your refrigerator full.

Why? If there is less space to cool, less energy is used.

132. Tip: Use natural cleaners for your fridge – like vinegar or baking soda and water.

Why? You will keep toxic chemicals in traditional cleaners out of your food zone.

133. Tip: Check the seal on your refrigerator door (you should not be able to pull a piece of paper out of the seal easily).

Why? A weak seal can leak energy and cost you money.

134. Tip: Get rid of aluminum pots and pans.

Why? Aluminum has been linked to Alzheimer's disease.

135. Tip: Keep a full pitcher of filtered water in your fridge.

Why? You will always have a supply of cold, clean water and it also keeps the fridge cool so you use less energy (kind of like how an ice pack works in a cooler).

136. Tip: Place low-E coated window film on your windows.

Why? The coating can reduce heat loss through windows by 40%.

137. Tip: Leave all shoes at the door.

Why? It will cut down on dust-bound pollutants and any nasties that you stepped in from getting into your home.

138. Tip: Seal your air ducts.

Why? The U.S. Department of Energy says that studies show that 10% to 30% of conditioned air escapes from ducts. Hire a professional service technician to test your system and fix any problems they find.

139. Tip: For outdoor lighting, buy solar lights.

Why? Solar lights recharge during the day, and then brighten your night – all for free.

140. Tip: Get a High Efficiency Particulate Air (HEPA) filter for your vacuum.

Why? They trap 99.97 percent of particles down to .03 microns in size. HEPA filters trap flame retardants, phthalates, and certain carcinogens and pesticides.

141. Tip: Don't get stain-proof treatments on carpets, couches, and car upholstery.

Why? They are loaded with toxic perfluoro chemicals.

142. Tip: Use kitty litter that has been made from plant sources like wheat or recycled newspaper.

Why? Clay-based litter is strip-mined, causing extreme environmental damage during extraction. Try www.yesterdaysnews.com.

143. Tip: Avoid zinc, lead, and copper containers, and use glass instead.

Why? They can make your food toxic or poisonous.

144. Tip: Use cleaning products that are made with plant-based biodegradable ingredients that have been packaged in bottles made from recycled content.

Why? They are better for the planet and your health.

145. Tip: Unplug your unused chargers.

Why? Chargers continue to draw electricity and waste energy and money.

146. Tip: Cover pots on the stove.

Why? You will avoid losing excess heat and wasting energy.

147. Tip: Open the oven door when you turn it off after you finish baking when it's cold.

Why? It will heat your home.

148. Tip: Find new uses for your old things.

Why? You will keep them longer and avoid buying new things.

149. Tip: Buy good quality things.

Why? They will last longer, and save money and resources.

150. Tip: Change your mattress to an organic one. Organic linens and pillows are great, too.

Why? Your current one may be full of chemicals and allergens.

151. Tip: Don't pre-wash dishes unless you really have to.

Why? You won't use water unnecessarily.

152. Tip: Use a reusable coffee filter instead of paper filters – at home and at work.

Why? You will eliminate paper waste and reduce pollution caused by the chlorine and other chemicals in the white paper.

153. Tip: Use bamboo servers in the kitchen.

Why? They are made from renewable resources, are beautiful. Check out www.bambu.com and www.branchhome.com, and www.surlatable.com. ☺

154. Tip: Buy recycled plastic mixing bowls and cutting boards.

Why? You will save resources and keep them out of landfills. Try shopping at Whole foods or look at www.recycline.com.

155. Tip: Get natural scrubbers for cleaning.

Why? They are better for you and the planet. Try www.kitchenkapers.com and www.peacefulcompany.com.

156. Tip: Get a Carbon Monoxide detector.

Why? You can't smell or see carbon monoxide, but high levels of it can kill a person in minutes.

157. Tip: Turn the pilot light on your fireplace off during warm summer months.

Why? You will save money and a lot of natural gas, which is resource-intensive during the process of extraction.

158. Tip: Eat with real dishes and silverware.

Why? They can be washed and reused, and the resources saved will start to add up quickly.

159. Tip: Don't buy bottled water – get a reusable BPA-free bottle and refill it with filtered water.

Why? Bottled water is a lot more expensive, uses many more resources to make, and gives off a lot of carbon emissions.

160. Tip: Keep things out of your home that will cause air pollution – cigarette smoke, chemicals, and excess moisture.

Why? They pollute the air in your home and can cause you and your family health problems.

161. Tip: Ventilate your home.

Why? You will pull dangerous pollutants out of the house. Running exhaust fans in the bathroom and kitchen, opening windows, and running the exhaust system in appliances and stoves will work wonders.

162. Tip: Test your home for Radon.

Why? Radon is the leading cause of lung cancer in non-smokers and the second-leading cause of lung cancer, period.

163. Tip: Clean your air-conditioner and dehumidifier.

Why? Standing water and high humidity encourage growth of dust mites, mold, and mildew.

164. Tip: Use a manual can opener, not an electric one.

Why? Unless you are disabled or suffer from arthritis, there is no need to waste the electricity needed to open a can.

165. Tip: Fill your home with plants.

Why? Plants can clean and negate the effects of harmful toxins.

166. Tip: Choose organic towels.

Why? They don't have any pesticides on them. Try www.ecobathroom.com.

167. Tip: Try natural dental care.

Why? No nasty chemicals for you to swallow. Check out www.tomsofmaine.com, www.naturesgate.com, www.radiustoothbrush.com, and www.thenaturaldentist.com.

168. Tip: Put a stop to credit card offers.

Why? They waste lots of resources, and end up in your shredder and recycling bin, anyway. Go to <u>www.opyoutprescreen.com</u>.

169. Tip: Reuse paper bags.

Why? They won't need to be recycled right away, can be used as animal cage liners, to hold shredded paper, and to wrap presents.

170. Tip: Rinse and reuse re-sealable bags.

Why? They are made from petroleum – reusing saves you from needing to buy more.

171. Tip: Bring your own coffee mug to fast-food restaurants.

Why? You won't have to bring the paper cup home with you to recycle with the other paper products they give you with your food.

172. Tip: Bring reusable mesh bags to the grocery store.

Why? You can put your produce in them instead of plastic produce bags.

173. Tip: Recycle plastic hangers.

Why? You will keep them out of landfills. Try <u>www.mvrecycling.com</u> if your town doesn't recycle them.

174. Tip: Instead of paper towels, try microfiber cleaning cloths.

Why? No paper and other resources wasted. Try www.methodhome.com.

175. Tip: Don't buy anymore plastic or wire hangers.

Why? They use precious resources to make them, and then they need to be recycled. Try Merrick Earthsaver hangers at Target and Walmart – they are made from corn and bamboo.

176. Tip: Have the delivery of phone books to your home and office stopped.

Why? It will cut down on paper and energy use. Go to www.YellowPagesGoesGreen.org and www.yellowpagesoptout.com.

177. Tip: Look into getting a greener energy provider.

Why? Renewable energy is better for the planet and can be easier on your wallet. Due to deregulation, many states now allow third party companies to offer greener energy at affordable prices. I use Viridian Energy which currently offers service in Il, NY, NJ, PA, MD, and CT.

Office

1. Tip: Recycle all of your paper and boxes, and buy recycled paper.

   Why? You will save trees and resources, and keep the paper out of landfills.

2. Tip: Print on both sides of the paper.

   Why? You will use half the paper, therefore half the trees, than if you print on only one side. Bonus tip: Use the back of other documents you no longer use, like flyers or your child's homework.

3. Tip: Stop the unwanted catalogs to your office and home.

Why? Every year, about 19 billion catalogs are mailed to American Consumers, according to The Daily Green. These catalogs require more than 100 million trees and 56 million gallons of wastewater to produce. Call the number on the catalog and ask to be taken off their mailing list or go to www.catalogchoice.org to opt out of more than 1,000 catalogs, and www.directmail.com.

4. Tip: Turn off your computer, monitor, and printer when you are not using them – especially at night. Use a power strip, and turn it off.

Why? It saves wear and tear on your hardware, not to mention the energy and money – up to around $90 per year. Turn off the monitor if it will not be used for over 20 minutes, and the whole computer if not used for 2 hours.

5. Tip: Pay your bills online.

Why? You will save stamps and can reuse or recycle the envelopes that come with the bill.

6. Tip: Have e-statements sent to you instead of paper statements.

Why? You will save resources, stamps, and time.

7. Tip: Don't sign up for mailing lists.

   Why? They will continue to send you mailings until you tell them to stop. Not getting them saves trees, other resources and energy.

8. Tip: Save as many documents as you can to your computer instead of printing them.

   Why? It will save paper, ink, and electricity.

9. Tip: Think twice before you print. Ask some questions first: Does it need to be printed? Are you printing on both sides of the paper? Can you save it to your computer?

   Why? You will save resources and money, and have less to recycle.

10. Tip: Download software.

    Why? There won't be any packaging or CD waste or resources used to produce them.

11. Tip: Use the power management mode on your computer.

    Why? Using the sleep mode with low power will save you around $75 per year and use up to 70% less energy.

12. Tip: Use a laptop or notebook instead of a desktop computer.

   Why? Laptops use more than 50 percent less energy than desktops and need fewer materials to make.

13. Tip: Use refillable pens.

   Why? Disposable pens are not biodegradable and end up in landfills – over a billion every year by Americans alone. Their parts and packaging are made from non-renewable resources and many contain nasty chemicals.

14. Tip: Work from home as much as possible.

   Why? You will save gas, money, and carbon emissions from going into the environment.

15. Tip: Skip the cute little coffee stirrers.

   Why? Americans throw away over a billion straws and stirrers every year. If you do use them, put them in the recycling bin.

16. Tip: Don't send a cover page with faxes. Write the persons name on the top if you need to.

   Why? You will save paper at both ends.

17. Tip: Use an eco-stapler for 5 pages or less.

   Why? They don't use metal staplers. Check out www.buyecostapler.com.

18. Tip: Teleconference.

Why? You will save time, money, and chemicals in the air by flying or driving to the meeting.

19. Tip: Shred receipts and recycle shredded paper.

Why? Bank, ATM, and gas pump receipts are often given automatically and should always be recycled. They have personal information on them, so for securities sake, shred them first, place them in a paper bag, and put them in your recycling bin. These receipts are a major source of litter. Say no to a receipt and save the paper!

20. Tip: If your company provides automatic deposits, sign up for it.

Why? You will reduce the time you spend, the gas you use, and get your money faster.

21. Tip: Green your workplace.

Why? You will spread your good ways and possibly lead others down the green path.

22. Clean the office water spigot regularly.

Why? People with germs on their hands or water bottle touch it and spread germs and colds.

23. Tip: Turn off your power strip.

Why? You will save electricity and money.

24. Tip: Recycle your ink cartridges and buy refilled cartridges.

   Why? It costs up to 75% less to make than new ones and saves resources.

25. Tip: Make scrap paper from used paper.

   Why? You won't have to buy more paper – saving money and resources.

26. Tip: Start a green team or green practices at work.

   Why? Others will become aware and choose to be more environmentally conscious.

27. Tip: Bring your own coffee mug.

   Why? Bringing your own cup eliminates the need to use disposable, and often non-recyclable cups.

28. Tip: Get an Energy Star-qualified computer.

   Why? They will go to a low power mode when they are not being used, reducing its energy use by up to 70% and extending its use.

29. Tip: Reuse or return packing peanuts, and avoid using them whenever possible.

Why? The expanded plastic is made from petroleum, they stay in landfills for hundreds of years, and they are harmful to marine wildlife and birds. You can return them to UPS stores. Use scrunched up newspaper or magazines, or try Papernuts, which are made from recyclable postconsumer cardboard at www.papernuts.com.

30. Tip: Don't use standard keyboard cleaners.

Why? They contain toxins – one 10 oz. can of chemical duster has the same greenhouse gas-creating effect as burning 100 gallons of gas. Just shake it and wipe it off.

31. Tip: Choose an LCD computer monitor over a CRT.

Why? They are more efficient – up to 66% more, according to the U.S. Department of Energy. LCD's are smaller in size, produce less heat, and are easier on the eyes.

32. Tip: Use tree-free pencils.

Why? They are made from 100% recycled newsprint. Get them at www.treesmart.com.

33. Tip: Use eco-paints to paint your office.

Why? To keep the air you breathe all day free of chemicals. Try www.afmsafecoat.com, www.americanpridepaint.com, and www.yolocolorhouse.com.

Environment

1. Tip: Say no to plastic bags.

Why? The EPA says that we use between 500 billion and a trillion plastic bags worldwide every year. Only 1 percent of these are recycled. They are made from polyethylene: a thermoplastic made from oil, they photo-degrade, and nearly 200 species of sea-life die from plastic bags – either by becoming entangled in them along our coastlines or by eating them – both nasty.

2. Tip: Use a reel (push) mower.

Why? Power mowers pollute the environment, are noisy, and can use more gas than your car! The pollution from running your power mower for 1 hour is equal to driving a car 350 miles. Check out www.reelmowerguide.com.

3. Tip: Calculate and reduce your carbon footprint.

Why? To determine and reduce the CO2 emissions you are responsible for. Calculate yours and learn how to reduce it at www.carbonfootprint.com.

4. Tip: Don't use gas leaf blowers.

Why? Gas leaf blowers pollute the air, waste gas, make lots of noise, and aggravate the lungs of people with asthma, other lung disorders and allergies. Get a rake and a yard waste bag or an electric or battery powered leaf blower.

5. Tip: Fertilize without pesticides. Go organic.

Why? You will keep nasty chemicals off your lawn and out of our water supply. Lead, mercury and cadmium are some toxic chemicals found in many fertilizers – don't put them on your lawn, especially if you have kids or pets. The NRDC says that more than 80% of the most commonly used pesticides today have been classified by the National Academy of Sciences researches as potentially carcinogenic, and are routinely found in mothers' milk. Find some good, homemade organic pesticides for your lawn at http://www.essortment.com/all/homemadeorgani_renu.htm.

6. Tip: Carpool whenever possible.

Why? The fewer cars on the road there are the better – you save gas, and don't pollute the air as much.

7. Tip: Steer clear of fireworks.

Why? They contain toxic chemicals that will rain down on you. Many fireworks produce dust and smoke that contain various heavy metals, sulfur-coal compounds, and other nasty chemicals. Some can cause respiratory and other health problems, and others, like barium, are poisonous and radioactive.

8. Tip: Buy produce from local farmers.

Why? The pesticides used on long distance produce to keep them fresh will not be on them, and you will support your local economy.

9. Tip: Pick up litter- especially bottles, cans, and paper- and recycle it.

Why? It gets put in its proper place.

10. Tip: Plan car trips.

Why? Doing many errands in one trip will save gas and money and keep your exhaust fumes less.

11. Tip: Ride the bus or train whenever possible.

Why? You will save money on gas and reduce CO_2 emissions.

12. Tip: Say no to water in restaurants if you won't be drinking it.

   Why? It's wasteful.

13. Tip: Find a green (wet) dry cleaner.

   Why? Most dry cleaners use a dry-cleaning solvent perchloroethylene (perc), a nervous system toxin and probable human carcinogen, according to the EPA. These chemicals end up in the water supply.

14. Tip: Don't let your car idle. Turn it off when you park.

   Why? An idling car emits much more pollution than a driving car and it wastes gas. Letting your car idle for 10 seconds uses more gas than turning it off, then on again. Americans waste around 2 billion gallons of fuel every year while idling.

15. Tip: Leave your grass clippings on your grass.

   Why? It serves as a fertilizer, and cuts down on organic fertilizer and water needs.

16. Tip: Use a digital camera instead of one that requires film or a disposable camera.

   Why? The solutions used to make prints contain hazardous chemicals that need to be disposed of specially. Most disposable cameras end up in landfills.

17. Tip: Avoid cruise ships.

    Why? Each ship uses several thousand gallons of fuel per hour. And then there is the waste they dump into the ocean – disgusting. ☹

18. Tip: If you have the option of taking a hybrid taxi, take it.

    Why? The exhaust emissions are much lower.

19. Tip: Never flush medications down the toilet. Find a drugstore or hospital that will dispose of them properly.

    Why? They wind up in waste-water that harms fish, plants, and animals, and also in our drinking water. Enter your zip code at www.earth911 to find a nearby drop-off site.

20. Tip: Looking for a new car? Buy a hybrid.

    Why? You will save CO_2 emissions, gas, and money.

21. Tip: Buy a partial zero-emission vehicle (PZEV).

    Why? They run around 90 percent cleaner than most new cars.

22. Tip: If you drive a vehicle that has a diesel engine, have it set up to use biodiesel.

Why? Biodiesel fuel is renewable, more energy efficient than other fuels, and doesn't contain sulfur pollutants.

23. Tip: If you want a motorcycle, get an electric or hybrid.

Why? Standard two-stroke motorcycles release around 25 times more pollution per mile than passenger cars do. Four-stroke engines save 25 percent on fuel, and cut emissions by 50 percent.

24. Tip: Drive less.

Why? Cars are responsible for around 60 percent of air pollution, which causes global warming, smog, and acid rain. Also, you will save resources and money. Try to plan errands along the route you are taking.

25. Tip: Stay on the ground, not in a plane.

Why? Planes spit toxic chemicals into the ozone layer, while most from the ground evaporate on the way up.

26. Tip: If you must fly, fly direct.

Why? Take-offs and landings use the most gas of your flight; take-offs consume around 25% of the total fuel on short flights.

27. Tip: Tune up your car.

Why? A car not properly tuned up produces 10-15 times more pollution than a properly tuned car.

28. Tip: Don't top off your gas tank.

Why? Topping it off allows excess fumes to be released into the air.

29. Tip: Obey the speed limit and maintain a constant speed.

Why? Speeding and rapid acceleration and braking can decrease fuel economy by 33%. Every gallon of gas you burn produces 19 pounds of carbon dioxide (25 pounds with the energy making and distributing it).

30. Tip: Have to go to the bank, or the pharmacy, or order some fast food? Walk in instead of using the drive-thru.

Why? You will save gas and carbon emissions by parking and turning off your car.

31. Tip: Don't litter.

Why? You will contribute to pollution, and probably feel really guilty about doing it, too.

32. Tip: Snip the plastic 6-pack rings before tossing them in the recycling bin.

Why? If they get into the environment, they can kill sea-life by entangling them, or they think they are food and eat them.

33. Tip: Don't water your lawn for long periods.

Why? For every hour you water your lawn, you use 330 gallons of water.

34. Tip: Buy biodegradable doggie-doo bags.

Why? Dog waste biodegrades in nature, but not if it's placed in a non-biodegradable bag, which takes around 100 years to decompose. Find them at www.ecoproducts. com.

35. Tip: Pour vinegar or boiling water on weeds.

Why? It will kill them without any harsh chemicals to harm the environment.

Recycling

1. Tip: Recycle your inkjet cartridges. Bring them to Office Max or Office Depot and get money back for doing so. ☺

   Why? It can take up to 450 years for them to decompose in a landfill, and it takes 80% less energy to re-manufacture plastic than make it new.

2. Tip: Save your old jeans.

   Why? When you have a few pair to donate, send them to Green Jean Insulation Inc. in Stoughton, WI where they make insulation from blue jeans. Go to their website at www.bondedlogic.com for more information.

3. Tip: Recycle more, throw away less.

Why? The average American creates about 4.5 pounds of trash every day. This trash is shipped to landfills. Try to limit your trash by recycling – newspaper, junk mail, cardboard, plastic and glass bottles, and cans. If all Americans recycled, 75% of waste would not be sent to landfills.

4. Tip: Recycle all paper, cardboard, and envelopes, and buy recycled paper. Practice this at home and at the office.

Why? According to the Sierra Club, an estimated 900 million trees are cut down annually to produce paper. Almost 50 percent of most American trash is paper. Buy recycled printer paper and sticky notes, print on both sides of paper, and buy recycled napkins, paper towel, plastic bags, toilet paper, paper plates, etc. For every ton of paper that is recycled, not fresh, we save 3,000 liters of water and 95% of the emissions.

5. Tip: Recycle batteries.

Why? Keeping them out of landfills is better for the environment and saves resources.

6. Tip: Recycle phone books and request that you are not to receive them.

Why? Telephone books make up around 10 percent of the waste in landfills. Save some trees. Try www. yellowpagesgoesgreen.com.

7. Tip: Recycle your cell phones – try your carrier, Office Depot, etc.

Why? If you put them in the garbage and send them to a landfill, the toxins in them, like mercury, lead, cadmium, arsenic and beryllium, can seep into the ground beneath them and contaminate the soil and groundwater. If they are incinerated, these substances will pollute the air. It also wastes raw materials.

8. Tip: Buy binders that have been made with recycled materials.

Why? You will reduce the amount of resources needed to make them.

9. Tip: Recycle old car tires, bike tires, and inner tubes.

Why? They can be used to make new boots, handbags, playground cover, etc.

10. Tip: Call your towns Department of Public Works.

Why? They will tell you what you are able to recycle and provide a recycling bin.

11. Tip: When you recycle plastic bottles, remove the caps.

Why? The bottle and the cap melt at different temperatures.

12. Tip: Check out www.earth911.org.

Why? They will tell you where you can recycle anything.

13. Tip: Buy milk in bottles if you have the option.

Why? They can be recycled – waxed milk cartons cannot.

14. Tip: Recycle plastic.

Why? It uses just 10% of the energy it takes to make a pound of plastic from virgin resources.

15. Tip: Recycle aluminum.

Why? Reusing aluminum is 95% more energy-efficient than creating products with raw materials.

16. Tip: Choose plastics #1, 2, 4, or 5.

Why? They are easy to recycle and don't contain nasties. Avoid #3, 6, and 7.

17. Tip: Avoid anything made from polystyrene (Styrofoam).

Why? They are made from petroleum and take eons to break down in landfills.

18. Tip: Recycle your cardboard toilet paper and paper towel rolls.

    Why? You will save resources and energy.

19. Recycle your old electronics.

    Why? Electronic waste (e-waste) takes up only 1% of our garbage, but contributes 70% of toxic materials in our landfills.

20. Tip: Recycle, donate, or share books.

    Why? It will save money and resources, and sharing gives hours of entertainment to the recipient of the book.

21. Tip: Buy products only in packages you know you can recycle.

    Why? It will save you guilt from having to send it to a landfill and is better for the environment.

22. Tip: Recycle cork from wine bottles.

    Why? You will keep them out of landfills and save resources. Check out www.recorkamerica.com.

23. Tip: Bring your bags from fast-food restaurants home with you. Always order to go.

    Why? You can throw it in the recycling bin. All of the garbage in fast-food restaurants ends up in landfills.

24. Tip: Recycle compact fluorescent light bulbs (CFL's).

Why? They can contain a small amount of mercury. Take them to a hazardous waste collection site, Ace Hardware, or Home Depot.

25. Recycle plastic straws.

Why? They will need to use fewer resources to make new ones – the plastic is already made.

Beauty

1. Tip: Buy a razor with refillable blades.

   Why? Disposable plastic razors can't be recycled and are not biodegradable. You will also save the resources required to make the plastic.

2. Tip: Skip the baby oil and choose oil made from the seeds of nuts and fruits.

   Why? Baby oil is a by-product of the production of gasoline.

3. Tip: Buy eyeliner pencils made of wood, not plastic.

   Why? The wood shavings will biodegrade, the plastic will not.

4. Tip: When you purchase make-up, consider its packaging before you buy it.

   Why? Some packaging can be recycled, others cannot. Some can be refilled, others cannot.

5. Tip: Choose make-up in glass containers over plastic.

Why? They can be recycled and save energy during manufacturing.

6. Tip: Buy lipsticks made with plant-derived ingredients, not those made from synthetic oils, paraffin waxes, and toxic coal dyes (F D & C or D & C followed by a color and number). Make sure they don't contain lead – toxic levels can build up in the body over time.

Why? You will save oil and they are non-toxic to you.

7. Tip: Examine the ingredients in your beauty products. Try natural or organic.

Why? Many beauty products have ingredients in them that may harm you. These nasties get onto your skin and go directly into your bloodstream. Check out www.cosmeticsdatabase.com.

8. Tip: The Environmental Protection Agency (EPA) suggests avoiding the following: Coal tar, fragrance, hydroquinone, Aluminum, triclosan, P-phenylenediamine, lead, and mercury.

Why? They contain chemicals that are carcinogenic, and many of them are neurotoxins and endocrine disruptors.

9. Tip: Go through your beauty products and throw away those with any ingredients from the previous tip.

    Why? They can harm you and should not be used again.

10. Tip: Avoid mineral oils (baby oil).

    Why? They coat the skin so it is unable to breathe, slowing down its cell development and natural functions. You may see it on labels as "liquid paraffin", or "petroleum".

11. Tip: Use natural oils to moisturize.

    Why? Natural oils, like olive, sweet almond, grapeseed, and jojoba oils, moisturize skin and hair, and are produced naturally.

12. Tip: Avoid parabens – chemical preservatives that begin with methyl-, ethyl-, propyl-, butyl-, and isobutyl-. Look for natural or organic brands, especially shampoo.

    Why? These chemical preservatives have been known as estrogenic and disruptive to normal hormone function. Always check the small print.

13. Tip: The term "fragrance" often hides a synthetic chemical called phthalates. Most fragrances are made from petroleum. Dibutyl and diethylhexyl have been banned in the European Union – not in the United States, though. Look for natural fragrances or no fragrance.

Why? They are known to cause birth defects, reproductive issues, and increased cancer risk.

14. Tip: Avoid Sodium Lauryl Sulfate (SLS) and Sodium Lauryl Ether Sulfate (SLES).

Why? The Environmental Working Group says they are carcinogens. Don't take the risk – avoid them.

15. Tip: Try to avoid the following: formaldehyde-producing preservatives, Benzyl and Isopropyl Alcohol, talc, and Silicone Derived Emollients.

Why? They can create the formation of carcinogenic chemicals. Check out www.safecosmetics.org or www.scorecard.org for chemicals profiles.

16. Tip: Skip the hairspray.

Why? Most commercial brands contain phthalates, alcohol, formaldehyde, polyvinylpyrrolidone plastic (a carcinogen) and fragrance.

17. Tip: Choose hair dye that is natural and doesn't contain any harmful chemicals.

   Why? Some of the chemicals are known to cause certain cancers. Try www.fruitfulyield.com.

18. Tip: Choose an eco-friendly bar soap.

   Why? They are better for you, your wallet, and the environment. Many contain detergents with synthetic lathering agents and harsh chemicals. The suds wash off you, down the drain, and into the water supply. Try www.sappohill.com and www.tspink.com.

19. Tip: For feminine products, order from www.seventhgeneration.com or www.natracare.com.

   Why? They are made chlorine-free, and Natracare is also organic.

20. Tip: Use a deodorant that does not contain aluminum.

   Why? It has been linked to Alzheimer's disease and may be associated with breast cancer – especially on freshly shaved skin.

21. Tip: Use sunscreens that are natural and organic.

Why? They don't contain nasty chemicals, like Oxybenzone, that will seep into your bloodstream and can cause hormone disruption, allergies, and cell damage. Try organic sunscreens at www.lavera.com, and www.drhauschka.com.

22. Tip: Instead of perfume, wear essential oils.

Why? Most perfumes can contain a mixture of around four thousand synthetic chemicals that have never been tested for safety. Many essential oils have anticeptic, antibacterial, antifungal, and preservative properties as well.

23. Tip: Avoid nail polish that contains formaldehyde, dibutylphthalate (DBP), phthalates, and toluene.

Why? These chemicals (in major brands) can cause birth defects, breathing problems, and cancer, among others. Buy soy- and corn- based or water-based nail polishes. Try www.pritinyc.com and www.suncoatproducts.com.

24. Tip: Avoid talc.

Why? It has been linked to ovarian cancer.

25. Tip: Use a nontoxic body/hair wash and diaper cream for your baby – that's about it. Target now carries an organic baby line called Erba Organics.

Why? Babies have natural oils to keep their skin moist. Give their water a couple drops of essential oil (I like lavender) if you want.

26. Tip: Make your own beauty products.

Why? You will know exactly what is in them, and save money, energy, and resources used for the packaging.

27. Tip: Use bar soap (some good ones at tip #18).

Why? No plastic bottles to recycle and no extra resources used.

28. Tip: Use fragrance-free personal care products.

Why? Fragrance may contain toxic chemicals.

29. Tip: Avoid hand sanitizers – especially those with triethanolamine and triclosan.

Why? Triethanolamine is a chemical that may damage the kidneys and liver, and they may cause more harm than good by killing beneficial bacteria as well as bad ones. Triclosan, an antibacterial/antifungal, disturbs hormones.

30. Tip: Buy refills for your pump lotion bottles.

Why? You will save money and resources in the production of the plastic.

31. Tip: Only use all-natural lip balms.

Why? No nasties that may harm you. Check out Blistex's organic Natural Cooling Comfort at www.blistex.com, Kiss My Face Lip Action at www.kissmyface.com, Shea Terra Organics Lip Butter at www.sheaterraorganics.com, and Earthlight Organics at www.earthlightorganics.com.

32. Tip: Buy make-up brushes made from renewable resources.

Why? They won't waste non-renewable resources to make them. Try brushes made with bamboo handles, taklon bristles, and recycled aluminum parts at www.ecotools.com.

33. Tip: Whiten your teeth with Hydrogen Peroxide.

Why? You will get whiter teeth without putting chemicals into your body and it is a lot cheaper than having it done at the dentist or store-bought kits. ☺

Green Living

1. Tip: Discover your local library.

   Why? Save trees and resources used in the production of books. Look for it in the library first. Borrow books, books on tape, videos, and CD's whenever you need them.

2. Tip: Donate old stuff.

   Why? Your old stuff at the back of the closet or in the basement can be donated and then purchased at a low price by others at the Salvation Army or Goodwill, it will stay out of landfills and you can write it off on your taxes.

3. Tip: Pack no-waste lunches. Use containers that can be reused.

   Why? It will save you (or your child) from having to throw away things that can be reused or recycled. Try www.kidskonserve.com/waste-free-lunch-kit/kkkita.htm.

4. Tip: Keep your tires inflated.

Why? Proper tire inflation improves your gas mileage.

5. Tip: Remove excess weight from your car.

Why? It will increase your gas mileage. Removable car racks reduce fuel economy around 5 percent.

6. Tip: Avoid rapid acceleration or slamming on the brakes.

Why? You will waste less gas and save money.

7. Tip: Send e-cards.

Why? It saves trees, resources, stamps, and time. Check out www.bluemountain.com .

8. Tip: Bring your own headphones on your airplane trip.

Why? The purchased set will probably end up in a landfill somewhere and it will save you a few bucks.

9. Tip: Capture rainwater in a rain barrel or bucket for gardens and plants.

Why? It's free water – saving you money since you won't be using your hose to water with.

10. Tip: Use a bucket instead of a hose if you wash your car at home.

Why? You will use less water and have less run-off water.

11. Tip: Go to a car wash instead of washing your car in your driveway.

Why? Most car washes recycle their water and the run-off doesn't go into the sewer and our water supply.

12. Tip: Plant an organic garden or grow fruits in your yard.

Why? You will know that they don't have any pesticides on them and it will save you money.

13. Tip: Grow your own organic herbs.

Why? You will know that they are organic and it will save you money.

14. Tip: Reuse your jars and containers.

Why? You won't have to buy more and recycle the old ones.

15. Tip: Share magazines.

Why? It will save resources and trees, and will save you and your friend's money.

16. Tip: Put back or save unused napkins.

Why? You will waste them. Keep some in your glovebox and spares around the house in case you run out.

17. Tip: Wrap presents in old calendar pages or comics from newspapers.

Why? You will save resources and money.

18. Tip: Give a donation to an environmental cause instead of a present (except for kids).

Why? You will support important causes.

19. Tip: Pass on the tissue wrap.

Why? You will save resources and money.

20. Tip: Make your next outfit vintage.

Why? You will save the energy and gas used in their production and transport.

21. Tip: Use a lunchbox, not a paper bag.

Why? They can be used over and over and over.

22. Tip: Put dry towels in the dryer with wet clothes.

Why? They will absorb wetness, cut down on drying time, and save energy.

23. Tip: Pick organic products when they are offered.

    Why? They will have no or less nasties in them.

24. Tip: Choose reusable instead of disposable products.

    Why? You will save money and resources, and not feel guilty that you will have to throw it away.

25. Tip: Take the stairs instead of the elevator.

    Why? You will save energy and get some exercise.

26. Tip: Avoid chemical flea collars.

    Why? They contain chemicals that can harm you and your pet.

27. Tip: Bring your own reusable bags to the store.

    Why? It will save you from having to recycle the paper or plastic bags they give you and give them the hint that people don't want them.

28. Tip: Use recycled toilet paper, paper towel, and napkins.

    Why? You will save trees, water and energy.

29. Tip: Get solar chargers for your cell phone.

    Why? They don't use electricity, only sunshine.

30. Tip: Bring your own garment bag for dry/wet cleaning.

Why? It will save you from having to recycle the plastic bag the garments will be returned to you in.

31. Tip: Bring hangers back to the dry/wet cleaners.

Why? Better to let them reuse them than to have them be recycled or thrown away (not by you, of course).

32. Tip: Ride your bike.

Why? You will save gas, not release any carbon emissions, and get some exercise, too.

33. Tip: Use matches instead of lighters.

Why? Over 1.5 billion lighters end up in landfills every year that were made from petroleum. Choose book matches over wood matches to save trees.

34. Tip: Use a soaker hose instead of a sprinkler.

Why? You can save up to 70% of the water you use to water your outdoor plants.

35. Tip: Get motion sensors for outdoor lighting.

Why? They only go on when something moves and turn off on their own.

36. Tip: Use your sprinkler in the morning or the evening.

    Why? It will help with evaporation.

37. Tip: Rent DVD's, don't buy them.

    Why? It will save you money and the time to find a DVD recycling center or a place to donate them.

38. Tip: Share popcorn.

    Why? To save money and packaging, share a bag of popcorn at the movies.

39. Tip: When you stay at a hotel, use the same towels and sheets the length of your stay.

    Why? The hotel will save up to 40% of its water use.

40. Tip: Take the bus.

    Why? Taking the bus instead of a car will more than double the distance you can go on fuel.

41. Tip: When you travel, pack lightly.

    Why? The lighter your luggage, the less fuel will be used to get you where you are going.

42. Tip: Print out maps on regular paper instead of buying a map.

    Why? Map paper can be hard to recycle because of the ink they use.

43. Tip: Skip the paper airline tickets and use e-tickets.

    Why? The airlines can save up to $3 billion every year by eliminating paper tickets.

44. Tip: Pack your own shampoo, soap, lotion, and toothpaste when you travel.

    Why? You will create less plastic waste by not using the hotel supply.

45. Tip: If you can, walk your child to school instead of driving them.

    Why? Walking doesn't waste any gas or create carbon emissions, and it is good exercise.

46. Tip: Buy your kids crayons made from soybean oil instead of paraffin wax.

    Why? Soybean wax crayons are non-toxic and not made from petroleum.

47. Tip: Don't buy food or snacks from vending machines.

Why? They have packaging that will most likely be put in the garbage near the machine.

48. Tip: Don't buy plastic made with polyvinyl chloride (PVC).

Why? PVC may contain toxins that can harm your immune system and is difficult to recycle.

49. Tip: If you have to choose between paper and plastic, choose paper.

Why? You can fit more in them, reuse them, and recycle them easier.

50. Tip: Buy in bulk.

Why? You will save money and packaging will be less.

51. Tip: Find local farmers markets.

Why? You will reduce the amount of petroleum used to transport your food by around 95% and you will support your local economy.

52. Tip: Choose fresh fruit over canned.

Why? You will save money on supplies, and save energy and resources.

53. Tip: If you eat meat, only buy what you need.

Why? More meat, resources (lots of water and petroleum), and money will be saved by cutting down or eliminating meat from your diet.

54. Tip: Buy clothes made from organic cotton.

Why? They don't use pesticides, herbicides, or fertilizers that will wind up in our environment and waterways.

55. Tip: Purchase shoes made from recycled materials.

Why? You will keep the waste from being put in landfills. www.sanuk.com

56. Tip: Buy pet toys, beds, collars, and leashes made from recycled materials, and make them canvas instead of nylon.

Why? Nylon production releases nitrous oxide – a greenhouse gas linked to global warming. Nasty.

57. Tip: Buy real Christmas trees instead of fake plastic trees.

Why? They can be replanted or recycled – no petroleum needed.

58. Tip: Look for recycled and recyclable wrapping paper and bows.

Why? You will save resources and trees.

59. Tip: Choose bottles over cans when buying beverages.

    Why? It will use a lot less energy to make them and better to recycle.

60. Tip: Buy organic wine.

    Why? You will keep pesticides and fertilizers out of the environment.

61. Tip: Before scheduling your next oil change, ask them if they use refined motor oil first.

    Why? Refined lubricating oil production uses fewer resources.

62. Tip: Try retread tires.

    Why? They use one-third of the petroleum resources to produce and cost less to buy.

63. Tip: If you are looking for a flat-screen television, choose a thirty-two inch LCD panel over an equal-size plasma screen.

    Why? They use a lot less energy.

64. Tip: Bring your own filtered water in a reusable bottle wherever you go.

    Why? You will know that the water is properly filtered and save resources and money.

65. Tip: Go outside to walk or jog instead of using a treadmill.

Why? You will save around sixty kilowatt-hours of energy per year. Oh, then there's the fresh air – ahhh…☺

66. Tip: Bring your own towel to the gym.

Why? You will save energy, and water, and you won't be exposed to any nasty chemicals your gym may use.

67. Tip: Swim in pools with saltwater (saline) or solar-ionized water instead of chlorinated pools.

Why? Pools sterilized with salts or ionization are better for the environment, your eyes, skin, hair, and lungs.

68. Tip: No synthetic nylon sponges.

Why? They are made from petroleum, can't be recycled, and are bad for the environment when they are disposed of.

69. Tip: Look for footwear with recycled rubber soles.

Why? You will save energy in their production and reduce waste.

70. Tip: Look for backpacks and duffel bags that are made from recycled materials.

Why? You will save resources and keep the plastic out of landfills.

71. Tip: If you are looking for a new bicycle, buy one with a steel frame instead of an aluminum frame.

Why? Steel frames can be made from recycled materials and save money in its production.

72. Tip: Buy used sporting equipment if possible.

Why? You will avoid using resources, money, and energy needed to make new stuff.

73. Tip: Don't buy gloves or mitts that are made from PVC plastic or vinyl.

Why? PVC is highly toxic when burned and uses a lot of energy to recycle. PVC production pollutes the air and water supply.

74. Tip: Use a yoga mat made from a plant-based material like cotton, jute, or natural rubber.

Why? The PVC in most yoga mats is environmentally toxic and can cause certain health problems. Use old yoga mats as doormats, put them under pet food bowls, etc. www.sunshineyoga.com, www.gaiam.com, wwwbarefootyoga.com

75. Tip: Try to avoid adhesives, or only select brands that are vegetable or water based.

Why? They contain chemicals that can be hazardous to your health – the vegetable and water-based adhesives can reduce the hazardous emissions by 99%.

76. Tip: Buy countertops made from recycled materials.

Why? You will keep around forty pounds of plastic out of the landfills.

77. Tip: Get a fuel-efficient and smaller car.

Why? You will save money on gas and reduce your carbon emissions.

78. Tip: When shopping, ask yourself, "Do I really need this?"

Why? You may save yourself some money and the resources used to make the item you are holding.

79. Tip: Don't buy anything for an entire day…then two days…then a week.

Why? You will buy less, only what you need, and save money and gas.

80. Tip: Instead of retail therapy, do some yoga, Pilates or go for a walk or run.

Why? You will save money and the resources needed to make the item you want to buy and feel better physically.

81. Tip: Never use mosquito repellents – especially if they contain DEET.

Why? They are highly toxic and poisonous. Use the essential oil citronella. Add some to your lotion before going outside – no bites!

82. Tip: If you have a particular item you need to buy, call the store first to see if they have it.

Why? It could save you the trip.

83. Tip: Try a water-less carwash.

Why? You will save the water and won't use any toxic chemicals.

84. Tip: Use the toilet at the airport before a plane trip.

Why? Each flush at 30,000 feet uses a quarter of a gallon of fuel.

85. Tip: Change your habits slowly – make a list and cross them off.

Why? You don't want to feel overwhelmed or stressed when you change. Start with recycling and turning off your car, adjust to it, then move onto something else, like saving water and changing your light-bulbs.

86. Tip: Talk about it.

Why? It lets the people in your home and life understand and hopefully support your choices.

87. Tip: Tune up your car engine.

Why? It can improve your car's fuel efficiency from 15-50%.

88. Tip: If you must fly, buy carbon offsets.

Why? They fund projects that will create clean energy, such as wind farms, solar plants, biomass facilities, etc., or to projects in sustainable development of emission-reducing initiatives.

89. Tip: Teach your kids why it is important to be environmentally friendly.

Why? They need to know how to protect the health of the only place they will ever live. Always set a good example for them.

90. Tip: Put on a sweater if it's cold.

Why? Keeping your heat low saves energy and money.

91. Tip: When it's hot outside, park in a shady spot.

Why? It decreases the amount of fuel that evaporates from the heat and you will use your air-conditioning less. The suns heat also causes toxins to evaporate from the fuel tank.

92. Tip: Go online less.

Why? Internet usage consumes about 400 billion kilowatts of energy per year.

93. Tip: Buy organic fruits and vegetables at the store.

Why? The organic sticker assures that the product is herbicide-, pesticide-, and fungicide- free.

94. Tip: Combine routine shopping trips with errands.

Why? You will save time, fuel, money, and emissions.

95. Tip: Be aware of greenwashing.

Why? Greenwashing is when a company sounds greener than they really are. An example: 100% postconsumer recycled box or 100% recyclable materials. The first is good, the second is greenwashing.

96. Tip: Wash and reuse plastic silverware, plates, cups, and baggies.

Why? You will save money, energy, and resources.

97. Tip: Avoid eating food from a can.

Why? Bisphenol A (BPA) is a toxic and carcinogenic chemical that coats the lining of canned foods and beverages.

98. Tip: Use a rain barrel or rain chains.

Why? Catching the water reduces the amount of rainwater that runs off your property and into overburdened sewer systems and gives you water for your plants, lawn, or garden. Saving money on your water bill is always good, too.

99. Tip: Use old clothes and towels for rags.

Why? You will save money and resources by not buying paper towel or sponges and they are reusable many times.

100. Tip: Use handkerchiefs instead of tissues.

Why? You can wash them over and over, and you will save trees.

101. Tip: Keep your car as long as you can, then buy a used one.

Why? Manufacturing just 17 new cars uses enough water to fill an Olympic-sized swimming pool, according to the Energy Information Administration.

102. Tip: Have a swap party with friends.

Why? You and your friends can all get new things without spending a penny or using resources.

103. Tip: Check with your local post office to see if they are part of the e-waste mail-back program.

Why? You can pick up pre-paid envelopes to send your e-waste to a third party to recycle it.

104. Tip: If you are in the market for a new washing machine look at front-loading machines that are Energy Star certified.

Why? Front loaders use one-third less water than top loaders, and are more effective and efficient.

105. Tip: Bring your own take-out container when you go to a restaurant.

Why? Most restaurants put your food in Styrofoam containers which become part of the environment after you are done with them.

106. Tip: Get a few space heaters.

Why? They will heat the area you are in and allow you to save money by keeping your heat down.

107. Tip: Close the vents in rooms you don't use regularly. Also, use a draft bag in front of the front door.

Why? You don't need to waste energy and money to heat rooms that are not used or because of drafts. Use a space heater to warm it up if it becomes needed.

108. Tip: Don't buy or use fun summer accessories like water wings, slip-n-slides, or kid pools.

Why? They are most likely made of polyvinyl chloride (PVC, or vinyl), which can contain phthalates and lead.

109. Tip: Replace multiple battery devices one battery at a time.

Why? Only one of the batteries may be dead. If you don't have a battery tester, get one.

110. Tip: Keep your batteries out of hot places.

Why? Heat may cause them to leak fluid.

111. Tip: Buy soy, beeswax, or palm wax candles.

Why? Paraffin wax candles release hazardous levels of benzene, airborne acetone, lead, tetrachlorethene, and carbon monoxide. Soy, beeswax, and palm wax are renewable and biodegradable, are non-petroleum based, and release far fewer chemicals than those made of paraffin wax.

112. Tip: Look for labels that say "USDA Certified organic".

Why? It means that at least 95% of the ingredients in it are certified organic and it doesn't contain synthetic petrochemicals.

113. Tip: Buy Fair Trade Certified food.

Why? This label ensures that farmers are paid fair, above market prices for their products and that their workers are paid fairly for labor.

114. Tip: Use a digital camera instead of disposable or film cameras.

Why? Disposable cameras will most likely end up in a landfill and processing regular film uses a lot of water, chemicals, and paper.

115. Tip: Put a stop to phonebook deliveries.

Why? The resources used to produce and distribute these books are enormous! Get on the "no deliver" list at www.yellowpagesgoesgreen.org to find local/regional directory pages publishers and tell them not to deliver to you.

116. Tip: Vote for changes and write letters to mayors and congressmen.

Why? Sometimes it's the best way to get things done.

117. Trade paperback books.

Why? You can save trees and money by swapping at www.paperbackswap.com.

118. Tip: Volunteer at your local conservation agencies.

Why? You will learn about and contribute to local conservation.

119. Tip: Buy or borrow pre-used or recycled moving boxes.

Why? You will save resources and money.

120. Tip: Look for reclaimed wood furniture.

Why? You save trees.

121. Tip: Learn to sew.

Why? You can make your own clothes and mend your gently used clothes.

122. Tip: Open the windows in your car and leave the A/C off.

Why? A/C can use around 20% of your cars gas.

123. Tip: Encourage local authorities to adopt sound environmental policies.

Why? You will help your immediate environment and your community to become more "green".

124. Tip: Get gift certificates instead of gift cards.

Why? The cards are made of plastic, zapping resources, and will stay in landfills forever.

125. Tip: Give a starter kit of eco-friendly gifts for holiday presents – include CFL lightbulbs, powerstrips, a tire pressure gauge, a BPA-free water bottle, and maybe even a water filter – and put it all in a canvas shopping bag.

Why? To get them started!

126. Tip: Remove unused roof and bike racks.

Why? It will reduce aerodynamic drag, resulting in better fuel economy.

127. Tip: Leave early, and don't rush around.

Why? It will save you from driving faster and breaking later, wasting gas.

128. Tip: Avoid peak traffic times.

Why? You will change speed less frequently and use less gas.

129. Tip: Close the sunroof and windows at high speeds.

Why? An open sunroof or window can increase aerodynamic drag and decrease gas mileage.

130. Tip: Donate extra or usable building materials to Habitat Restores.

Why? They help local affiliates fund construction of homes in the community being built by Habitat for Humanity. Find out about it at www.habitat.org.

131. Tip: Buy non-toxic markers and crayons.

Why? They are better for your health and for the environment. Try www.auspenmarkers.com and www.prangpower.com.

132. Tip: Donate leftover paint to local places in need –
     charities, high school, drama departments, Habitat
     for Humanity, etc.

Why? They will get used by places that need them.
Look for nearby places at <u>www.earth911.org</u>.

Resources

1. www.earth911.com

2. www.thedailygreen.com

3. www.treehugger.com

4. www.gorgouslygreen.com

5. www.epa.gov

About The Author

Kim Cecchi is a mom, environmental activist, writer, Personal Fitness Trainer, and yoga and fitness instructor.

Being a mom has inspired her to care for the place where her, her child and (hopefully) grandchildren, friends, and family will live their lives.

Being an environmental activist has inspired her to share everything she has learned about caring for the environment with everyone.

Being a writer has given her the chance to share her knowledge, thoughts, and ideas with the world.

Being a yoga and fitness instructor for over 20 years has enabled her to help others care for themselves – physically and mentally, and through her newsletters, environmentally.

Please feel free to send comments, such as finding typos, or if you found the book helpful, or if you have any questions to Kim Cecchi at gettinggreen@comcast.net.